Settled for the Night

Settled for the Night

Poems

Ralph Stevens

RESOURCE *Publications* · Eugene, Oregon

SETTLED FOR THE NIGHT
Poems

Copyright © 2026 Ralph Stevens. All rights reserved. Except for brief quotations in critical publications or reviews, no part of this book may be reproduced in any manner without prior written permission from the publisher. Write: Permissions, Wipf and Stock Publishers, 199 W. 8th Ave., Suite 3, Eugene, OR 97401.

Resource Publications
An Imprint of Wipf and Stock Publishers
199 W. 8th Ave., Suite 3
Eugene, OR 97401

www.wipfandstock.com

PAPERBACK ISBN: 979-8-3852-6805-4
HARDCOVER ISBN: 979-8-3852-6806-1
EBOOK ISBN: 979-8-3852-6807-8

VERSION NUMBER 01/05/26

For Sydney Landon Plum
In friendship and gratitude.

Great Nature has another thing to do
To you and me; so take the lively air,
And, lovely, learn by going where to go.
—THEODORE ROETHKE

Contents

Acknowledgements and Thanks | xi

Prologue

Skunk at Dawn | 3
Imperfect Judgment | 4
Allegory | 5
To All That Lives | 6
How to Lose Your Mind | 7
At Peace with Darkness | 9
A Meditation in a Time of Healing | 10

I

Penetrating as Rain | 15
Over Her Shoulder | 17
The Poppy | 18
Refuge in a Photograph | 19

II

At First I Wait | 23
This Uncertain Storm | 24
Northeaster | 25
Top Withens | 26
Waiting above Me | 27

III

An Ordinary Day in June | 31
That Small Flotilla | 32
Arboretum | 34
Burning Trash | 35
Too Old for Love or War | 36
Alexa | 37
The Door Handle | 38

IV

Endless Light | 41
Something Not Found | 42
Driving at Night | 43
Reading at Dawn | 44
Into Sunlight | 45
The Photograph | 46
And Never Spent | 47
Without a Sound: Variations on a Theme | 48

V

The Wheelhouse | 51
Night Watch | 52
Island Road | 53
The Trout Hatch at the Winery | 54
Damp Wood | 55
Independence Day, July 4, 2022: The Deer Sleep | 56
Waking Up | 57
Cooperation | 58
After the Election | 59
A Valentine for Ash Wednesday Falling on February 14, AD 2024 | 60
The Calendar | 61
A Certain Point | 62
What Binds Us to History | 63

VI

Unfinished Picture | 67
Inflamed | 68
The River Is Not Responsible | 69
Silent in a Winding | 70
Deeply Hidden | 72
Out of Bounds | 73
That Death Is Looking | 74
Content to Pause | 75
Settled for the Night | 76
Envoy: Lyric, Sometimes Quiet | 77

Acknowledgements and Thanks

Crab Creek Review for "Night Watch."

Deep Water for "The Photograph."

Red Wolf Journal for "At Peace with Darkness" and "The Door Handle."

Sheila Na Gig for "Into Sunlight," published as "Some Sort of Ghost."

The Island Reader for "How to Lose Your Mind" and "Lyric Sometimes Quiet." "Lyric Sometimes Quiet" was subsequently published in *Pittsburgh Poetry Houses, Verse-Virtual, Gyroscope Review,* and on the radio program *Journey Daily with a Compelling Poem.*

Verse Virtual for "A Meditation in a Time of Healing," "And Never Spent" (published as "Mercy"), "Cooperation," "Over her Shoulder," "Penetrating as Rain," "Waiting above Me," "Without a Sound."

SPECIAL THANKS ARE DUE to the following for their help and influence in the making of this book: my readers, Jeanne Kohn and Elizabeth Phelps, for careful attention and insightful comments; and my wife, Sally Rowan, for her expert editing of the manuscript. It goes without saying that the positive influences on the writing of a book are too numerous to track but I would be remiss not to mention the encouragement of fellow poets Betsy Mars and Alan Walowitz, and Jim Lewis, editor of *Verse Virtual.*

Prologue

Skunk at Dawn

I wake early, and look around
for what the world might send,
of wonder, perhaps, or just a few
bars of song, but
the only tune I'm offered
is the lullaby of sleep,
an invitation to hit the pillow.
And I could RSVP, except
the lingering scent of last night's
anxious skunk hangs over the bed.
The world says, "Here
is something to wonder at,
a fact as unavoidable as it is
independent of your yawns."
So I wonder. What do I have in common
with a creature who makes a stink,
if only for protection?
Is that what we share,
the need for safe haven,
mine of sleep, skunk's of odor?
Protection from what? I'd appreciate
shelter from this smell,
raw, unwelcome, offensive.
Such odors don't invite collaboration
between skunk and me, but in itself
that is a sort of wonder.
The skunk and I share little,
separated as we are by what's
acceptable to the nose.
Might there be common ground
where we could meet, skunk and I,
somewhere past this nosy barrier?
That would be something
to wonder at.

Imperfect Judgment

It can be enough sometimes,
however imperfect.
The serve was good although
the line ump called a fault.
The match goes on.
The stew has just a bit
more salt than it needs.
It's edible. Creation is not,
as many wish, a Swiss watch.
The planets wobble, poles shift
as the centuries pass and
an innocent man
reads in his cell,
    innocently waits,
        makes the most of
            the time left to him.

Allegory

I ask to be excused to dream,
of a schooner voyage, or
if that's inexcusable,
to be allowed to drift like Huck
on a raft, a canoe.
Dreams are what we poets
hold fast to, until we're found out,
idle drunkards of the fantastic.
So we abandon ship
for the crusty alleys
of some ragged seaport
where dreams are seen
for the hollow hope
they are, a front for
frustrated desires.
Even so, I thought I'd
be happy there
on that schooner,
watching the main sheet
tighten as the deck rolled leeward
and I grabbed the railing.
But it gave way,
and I fell headlong
into the schooner's wake.
It was not the time,
as I rose gasping to the surface,
to wonder whether dreams
might not always be
the proper stuff of poetry
after all.

To All That Lives

I sit and contemplate the sounds
that wrap themselves around me as I sit,
the rapid pulse a motorcycle makes
as it recedes down the street,
the crows' insistent chatter in the trees,
claiming the territory for their own.

My mind in all this wants to break away,
shake off these wrappings, crack the shell and fly,
the way the mind can, even though the room
is warm, the chair that holds me firm, intent
on keeping me just where I am. There are
other thoughts, and I listen
to things that live and move in thought,
the boy who walks the sand and talks aloud,
knowing the sea listens, horses
who seem only to graze, but
in that grazing make a pact
with every blade of grass.

I could go on,
the mind elastic, welcoming
the near and distant,
generous to all that lives,
the field mouse in her hole,
the kindly earth that shelters her,
and the crows,
    though I may not always know
        what they're saying.

How to Lose Your Mind

Do it where the road turns
sharply on an afternoon so bright
the sun lasers off a stretch of ocean
un-cornered suddenly.
While you wince and blink, your mind jolts loose,
leaves you in the car.
Let it go, balloon tugged free,
Rocking skyward over surf.
Let it settle out of sight,
beyond the breakers, where
it won't be yours at all, but gone,
through sanity of eye and bone,
whiter than the walls of clinics,
to a beach on an island
where gulls tear mussels out of kelp,
drop them cracking,
moist and succulent
on the rocks.

Then mind would be a place to visit,
if you safely read the clouds before you start,
the boat strong with the smell of fish and diesel.
Bring a friend, one to help make fast
at the old dock, walk the shore,
stiff sea grass cutting your ankles,
to carry driftwood that you'll never use
to make that lampstand for the cottage.
You could collect the shells and spruce cones,
sea bird's skull, salt-cured upon a log,
the ocean light tempting you to think
it's yours again,
this beach wrack of a mind,
crab face hanging from a bleached stick,
signaling the kingdom

on the other side of madness,
free of time and prophecy,
and open a few weeks in summer.

At Peace with Darkness

The silence loved by monks,
a path in the woods after rain.
Small dips and hollows now puddled
soak the unwary foot.
So with the silence of this walk,
the space it makes for musing.
Perhaps you were only
making a list in your head when
you almost missed the baby rabbit,
thinking it was a rock, but
there it is. You made it freeze,
you with your clumsy feet,
the rabbit, with its red eyes
seeing what you miss.
But then you do,
the small rock bunny,
waiting, unmoving, waiting
for you to make the first move.
You need only become,
for the moment,
the monk at one with silence,
at peace with darkness,
before you walk on.

A Meditation in a Time of Healing

After a while the waves subside,
Become a stroking of the sand,
Swirl around the rocks,
A mere chuckle in the sea's throat.

And the sea herself
Softens to the mother
Our bones have
Told us she is,

As she is in this calm mood
When the gulls relax from
Swooping and diving
After morsels on the beach,

Begin their slow watchful
Strut and the dog no longer
Races the flock of terns
Across the shining flats.

He shakes himself into
An easy trot beside us
While the young
Fisherman whose arm

Found the jaws of a winch,
Yet managed to hang on
While his mates
Got him to shore,

Watches the harbor,
Boats unloading the day's catch.
Somewhere deep the hope lay
Through hours of intensive care,

Among the dripping tubes,
Ticking monitors, the hope
Of this fisherman that
The strong limb was there

Along with the
Beating heart,
With blood born
From the sea's brine

And would appear again,
In his healing.

I

Penetrating as Rain

With hey, ho, the wind and the rain...
—TWELFTH NIGHT

Is this what it all comes down to,
the thing called loss?
And not just the weeping
on a cold January night.
You thought
everyone was tucked in,
sleeping, but there it is,
faint and
penetrating as rain.

Loss can be an ordinary
stop light, red for a few moments,
and on you go. You've lost
a little time,
but then the light changes.
You put the car in gear,
and get it back.

"I lost my mother's watch,"
the poet writes. How is it
loss can be that small and
easy to master, yet sometimes
reduce you to tears?
The rain, it raineth every day,
and you expect the big calamity.

Then the sun comes up, and gladly,
while the broken marriage,
the creep of dementia,
wait in the wings.

You don't always hear
that low sound,
which might actually be
someone weeping.

Over Her Shoulder

After Louise Penny's A Brutal Telling.

She walks toward the front door,
opens her purse for the keys.
This is where life
pauses each day,
in a house surrounded by the ancient elms,
carefully tended garden,
the house where in a moment
she will put away groceries,
put on some music
and open a bottle of wine.
She thinks about what to have for dinner,
thinks about the children
getting off the bus, their father
opening the garage, all the
safe, familiar things. But that
moment is yet to come.
Now she turns,
looks over her shoulder.
It's still there,
what each day arrives with her,
the old sorrow that
follows her into the house.

The Poppy

In Flanders fields, the poppies blow
Between the crosses, row on row...

—JOHN MCCRAE

After the missile attack,
in the rubble where a bent
bicycle waits for the boy
to lift it home, where
sheets of broken plywood lie
ready to become shelter
for a mother and her three-year-old—
in a no man's land now home
to a ravaged people—
the poppy, which has no power
to name what has happened,
waits for spring, waits
to show its brilliant colors,
    sunny yellow, orange, peach,
       even blue.
           And sometimes red.

Refuge in a Photograph

I read the sad account
of evil done to good people,
and take refuge
in a photograph.
A stricken tree leans
across the woodland path,
as if to say, "Please.
Don't bring your sorrow here
among the trees."
I've done my share
of walking in the woods,
have lowered myself
beneath a guardian tree.
I bend now,
enter the picture,
charmed by the trail,
its pine needle pavement,
how it turns like the turnings
of a plainsong chant,
accommodates the wanderer.
Roots across my way could be
goblins sent to trip me
but I'm in no hurry.
I follow the turns,
respect the earth's right
to a certain unevenness,
to subside now and then
around a rock.
There's enchantment here and
not only in the gentle way
of woodland paths.
These trees tell me to lose all fear,
the way children
escape the cruel stepmother

and hide in a forest,
find a magic door.
I join them and
    we open it,
        together.

II

At First I Wait

If I plunge into those trees,
lunge ahead too fast,
I could find myself,
before I know it,
ankle deep in a dark
bog of wet moss, stuck
and wondering what I've missed.
Am I lost in this forest?
Is it haunted?
The path is soft and tells me
there is something still ahead,
something that wants to be found.
    "And it will be
        if you take it slowly."
So I do. The trees,
quiet because they listen,
affirm each step that is
honest and just. I keep on
in imitation of their sincerity,
    stop looking,
        expect nothing
except there is this steady trail this
wise forest.
It opens onto
a rocky shore, waves,
a tide running, an ocean
beyond irony and doubt,
    washing away
        all darkness.

This Uncertain Storm

In this uncertain storm
unsure of its plans,
how it will end
or if it will.

In this uncertainty
of wind, of leaves
torn from their roots
and flying,

this uproar
of scudding cloud
shaking walls
lights winking.

In this upending day
of time spun counter-
clockwise, looking
where to rest,

is a shelter
dug with each breath
and furnished
by the storm.

Northeaster

Halfway down the stairs I stop.
The house is empty.
A curtain sways
gently at the landing.
On an ordinary day
I wouldn't notice, but
the sky is falling,
heavy with the thunder
of surf at Bunker Cove.
This storm will not grow old.
The phone is dead.
I cannot call my wife to say
    the one thing
        on my mind
            right now,
the way her hair feels,
    warm when sunlight
        falls on it.

Top Withens

Should you come here on a summer's day,
the four mile walk across the moors
might seem nothing, a light
romantic fancy, ramble
through the heather on the hills.
At the ruin of the old house
you hear no wuthering around corners,
through empty window holes,
among the ghosts of another time,
another season.
For that you'll come
a few months later, in November
with a colder wind tugging
at your jacket, threatening
to take your hat.
Sit in one of the roofless alcoves
and if your mind permits
you might hear
not just the voice
of a haunted wind,
but of a solitude,
a loneliness even,
that cannot be broken,
not within this bleak stone house, nor
try as you might,
on the miles of moorland
waiting outside.

Waiting above Me

And I feel above me the day-blind stars waiting with their light.
—WENDELL BERRY

And they teach us to await
what we all wait for,
with the frog in the marsh,
singing for a mate, with gulls
landing together on the lake.
For an end to pain
in the bended knee, and
the beginning of summer.
For the savory pot roast
to arrive at the table, for dawn
to arrive in the sleepless night.
To wait like shepherds,
watching their flocks
under the waiting stars.

III

III

An Ordinary Day in June

Today my daughter turned thirteen.
Other than that it was
an ordinary day, a day in June,
with all the June paraphernalia—white clouds,
blue sky, sunshine. Except that I forgot this is
the coast and in these northern latitudes
we get a lot of fog in June. The cool
breeze off the ocean blows it in, sometimes
without warning, in the afternoon just when
we're sitting down to deviled eggs, hot dogs
and chips, at the picnic table near the rocks.
No matter. We'll just go inside, perhaps
light a fire, drive off the chill and play
Monopoly for a while. The sun
might burn the fog off later,
though this chill feels like
the staying kind.
We'll take it. There's a good
stack of maple for the stove, and yellow-page
Agatha Christies from the attic.
They'll keep us occupied, and after all
I said it was an ordinary day in June,
except, of course, my daughter turned thirteen.

That Small Flotilla

Sitting in the stern, I
drink my morning coffee
and count the goslings as they
follow their mother
across Portage Bay.

And there's one less.
I know, because I
count them every day
of what's left
of my own days.

"Do you know,"
I ask their mother,
"that you've
lost a child, lost her
to some hungry seagull?"

And of course she knows,
in the way of wild things,
as she knows all of their lives,
how well they swim and when
they'll be ready to fly.

This mother does not
look behind her, check
that small flotilla
of tiny goslings.
There is, in mothers,

knowledge of the law of
"Watch your children,"
or they'll be lost

to that law's blind justice.
Yet I think,

a child's now gone and
what will that mother do next?

Arboretum

appareled in celestial light...
—WORDSWORTH

I didn't know the kingfisher,
that he spells his name in diving,
that the heron speaks
an immense elegance
as he rises from the marsh.
A one-year-old is not
a knowing creature, although
    he sees celestial light,
        how it shines on the grass,
           the trees of the arboretum.

It was a world that
came to me where I was,
at the age I was,
unthinking and when
    words were
        beside the point.

Today I retrace my steps,
look for that arboretum, hoping
to recover its green thought,
stand at the river,
watch the kingfisher catch fire.
In age, I have
ears to hear the croaking heron,
    to listen
        for the quiet conversation
           of the trees.

Burning Trash

I was in the field burning trash
when the geese flew over,
leaving for the warm marshes
of the Chesapeake.
Earth-bound beside the black
circle of earth, site
of this domestic routine,
all I could do was look up.
Where was I in that moment?
Grounded with the fire or
transformed, airborne and
flocking with the geese?
It was the fire that brought me back to earth
where it had claimed its liberty,
flown into the surrounding grass,
September-brown now,
dry with age.
But the flames were young,
quickly disciplined by my shovel
while the geese flew on,
indifferent to a boy's longings,
and crying freedom.

Too Old for Love or War

The eyes of men
Too old for love or war
Follow a crow into the woods.

The woods, they think,
Are dark and deep,
A mystery.

They think how life
Lies in woodland pools
After the rain.

Now a doe
Comes down to drink
While the old men watch.

And then there are
Two, four, six crows,
A family in the trees,

And a herd of deer,
Looking back
At the old men.

The deer are not
Afraid. The eyes
Of the old men

Mirror the woods,
Crows in the tree tops.
The eyes of the deer.

Alexa

I have a house guest,
Alexa.
The kids insisted,
as adult kids will,
when a parent grows old,
and is a falling risk.
But what do those kids of mine
think Alexa will do when
I'm lying on the floor,
gasping, struggling
to remember her name?
"Alexa!" I finally manage but
she doesn't hear me,
and the kids
are all at home in Cleveland
shopping online or
watching TV.

The Door Handle

What does she think as she
reaches for the door handle,
above, almost beyond
her tiny hand? Is she curious
about what might be
on the other side?
She is too young to fear
the big bad wolf or,
worse, the corrupt judge,
venal politician.
This door opens on possibility
and the possible is
everything a child dreams of,
things bright with color, swift
with twists and turnings,
with fireflies, starlight and ponies,
while the wolves sit quietly
beyond her young years.
Of course, a child's vision
being what it is,
on things immediate,
right in front of her, all this
could just be my imagination.
My dreams are,
after all,
just my own.
She sees a door handle,
pure and simple,
a gleaming pebble which,
itself alone,
makes her joy complete.

IV

Endless Light

Wind northwest and
on the lake, waves
are a school of fish,
flashing in the afternoon sun.
It's still daytime and,
although night will come,
this day insists on fish,
on wind and waves,
on endless light.

Something Not Found

The night offers
something not found
in a closed room.
How might we dream
if we sleep outside
with the breeze from the pines
to fan our faces?
In the morning, dew
collects on our blankets.
We face an open sky,
watch the stars dissolve,
and see what we have become
while sleeping
this close to the night.

Driving at Night

Driving at night what might I find,
or would I care when I found it?
There is the air
through the open window,
the night odors of wet leaves,
low song of tires.
I am joined by eyes
that flash in the headlights,
watch me pass in the dark,
    something I share, with them,
        with all solitary things,
        driving at night.

Reading at Dawn

I cannot can say what chance
arrangement put me here at dawn,
to listen to the old clock
swing its pendulum
through tick and tock,
to read a few poems.
The Afghan turned loose
when my wife went up to bed
tells me nothing, although
who can say
     the arrangement
        is by chance?
But I have this solitude,
    these poems.

Into Sunlight

Is it some sort of ghost,
the thing we call grace?
It's hardly visible,
appears unannounced, quietly,
a cat walking across bare floor,
flutter of a bird's wing.
Words come now and then, unpredictable,
signs of grace arriving,
a break in the clouds.
The cat was sleeping on the radiator
until she woke and
jumped down into sunlight,
into pulsing footfalls and from there
to the milk.
I do not question her. Grace is
the unasked-for circle of a life,
and tends, animal-like,
toward simple things,
a bowl of milk,
sunshine on the floor.
And these words
that proceed with ease,
as from the wingbeat of a gull,
the footfall of a cat
just now awake.

The Photograph

In the distance, the green hump
of an island, and here,
blue water and
the bow where my children sit,
laughing as salt spray flashes,
up and into their bright faces.
But this is just a photograph,
trying to close the distance
between past and present,
create a memory.
It's what we ask photographs to do,
catch the light of a moment
and make it fast, a boat
at some dock of the mind.
We've been at sea for
years now, it seems.
I hold the picture,
talk to those children.
Did we,
I ask them,
ever make it
to that island?

And Never Spent

The world is charged with the grandeur of God.
It will flame out, like shining from shook foil...
—GERARD MANLEY HOPKINS

And the same, I thought,
could be said of the mercy of God,
not always shining, alight with flame,
but glowing, the ember
shook loose by the poker.
That alert pedestrian,
helping an old woman through the door,
father consoling a child,
her sobs fading along with the pain
of a skinned knee.
Oh, the world has its grandeur,
its monster glaciers,
mountain peaks,
vast lakes and oceans,
but there's a grandeur of sorts
in the small skiff, tied to the dock,
waiting for a boy, oars on his shoulder,
in the shopping cart of canned goods
for the homeless shelter, in any family
gathered by the TV on a winter evening.
Grandeur meets mercy in small things,
unnoticed by kings and presidents,
tiny in scale, but still divine,
as grand as snow-covered fields,
the shook foil of northern lights,
a steady glow,
and never spent.

Without a Sound: Variations on a Theme

With thanks to Emily Dickinson and James Wright.

Where I walked,
    it was all sky, and
        all water.
I could not be sure, and
    did it matter?
There seemed to be no
boundary, no limit, it was
an expanse of light,
a splashing ocean,
    all beyond, above,
        a canyon of sunlight,
            green afternoon without end.
I rowed with only light for oars,
    dividing seamless
        the silver, the gold
            along the banks of noon,
and soft, softer,
    without a sound.

V

The Wheelhouse

The wheelhouse is where he watches
while the ship swings slowly at anchor
in the current of the great river.
Where he reads the lights
of passing vessels, listens for the radar
to ping the presence of tug or tanker
inside the danger zone.
The night slips away and
light slowly arrives. He
lays a hand on a book
starts to turn the pages
in the glow of instruments.
Words will bridge the hours until
his relief comes aboard, will sing
the long slide of the Mississippi,
the numbness of a night watch,
will reach from the wheelhouse
to his driveway,
to the kitchen where his wife stands
humming while she makes the coffee
and the sun comes up.

Night Watch

Her shoes sprawl on the carpet,
dirt brown, scuffed,
collapsing inward like a fallen cake.
Across the room
she fills her chair like a tired foot
takes ease in an old shoe. She has
pruned Swedish Ivy, bridled
wandering Tradescantia, exorcised
all chrome and plastic from her house.
She favors wood, the color peach,
dried flowers in a cool blue jar.
Baskets on the wall file errata:
loose matches, mail, tobacco.
A bird's nest holds
a hill of herbs and spices, the room
aromatic, like an anointed lover.

Or like a musty sleeping bag, I tell myself,
the one she drags down here each night at ten.
Wearing it she spreads
a larval comfort on the couch,
conjuring a dark Sierra
where the eyes beyond the fire fade to stars,
where her great aunt pins her skirts
and walks a marsh by moonlight,
is said to be a witch.
She gives me *Beauty and the Beast*,
a whale's bone, and a card
that pictures two treed cats,
stark on a narrow limb,
loving every minute of the night.

Island Road

We knew it,
long before it had that name.
Knew it hot in July, its dust
coating the leaves of oak
and poplar saplings.
Knew it in the January snow,
deep between forest banks.
We'd get up in the early hours,
blizzard howling,
and start plowing before plowing
became impossible.
It was there, the road, for walking
to the mailbox at the crossroads,
across the causeway to the island,
through the marsh
where we might watch the tide
flood the road.
Some days I might
walk with my sister,
arriving at the edge of the woods
to see house and barn spread out,
a home beyond the hay fields.
We knew it as
the only ones who ever rode
or walked or plowed but,
it was just the island road.
We never thought
to give it a name.

The Trout Hatch at the Winery

At Chateau Ste. Michelle the goldfish hang
in blue enameled bowls among the roses.

Shutters are wine dark and slender. Trucks
unload beneath two Romanesque arches.

We walk past ornamental vines, and for lunch
choose crackers, Gloucester cheese and Chenin Blanc.

At the pond geese swim up, aloof and begging,
their long necks snaking down to gulp at scraps.

A heron cocks his prehistoric head,
flaps off on mammoth wings. Later we find,

shadowed by hemlocks, a small hatchery,
and trout spawn, swarming in silent pools.

Damp Wood

My friend lives in a small city,
and has a skunk issue,
a skunk outside the window,
doing his night things.
"I was," she told me,
"at war with this skunk,
but with no weapons."
A war she was always losing
while the skunk
perfumed the window.
He was hungry, feeding on grubs
that lived in the wood pile
stacked below.
"So I shipped that skunk smorgasbord
to another yard," she said.
"Now I open the window
to the sweet night air."
Meanwhile those grubs,
indifferent to their new location,
or the appetite of skunks,
just pursue their love affair
with that pile of damp wood.

Independence Day, July 4, 2022: The Deer Sleep

It doesn't take much
to explain Independence Day,
not to the peepers in the marsh next door.
Their mating calls
announce their freedom
to find a lover for the night.
The deer claim no right
to bed in the tall grass.
They simply lie down
after a day spent grazing
among the neighborhood trees.
And the skunks. They
don't seem troubled by their
unsavory reputation but,
like the deer,
take their nourishment
where they find it,
    then go to sleep,
        under the shed behind the house,
            indifferent to the fireworks.
They don't celebrate their independence,
any more than does the groundhog
grazing freely now
    outside the window
        where I sit at liberty
            and write this poem.

Waking Up

The rooster crows as I sit writing,
    then stops.
Perhaps he knows I heard,
perhaps he knows silence
    is what I need.
Or is this all just fancy,
playing with the mind
of an unminding chicken?
I have other cries to listen for,
    the night bird's call,
        the lover's breath.
Why wake up to a raucous,
rooster-scolded day?
Or, for that matter, wake
    to darkness,
        to the skein of half-sleep
            stretched across the bed?
Let me wake to the fires of time
    and welcome their slow burning.

Cooperation

The crocus lies under the snow for as long as it takes,
then appears (all too briefly)
to suggest a promise
in which our cooperation is required.

—COMMENT FROM A FRIEND

And it can take a while
for the crocus to appear,
while the shadow of a tree,
its fulness flattened
makes uneven patterns
of grays, of gaps between the grays
on my neighbor's house.
The pattern shifts
as the sun shifts
but slowly, giving me
time to read there
a promise.
The world is full of such,
gaps between the shadows,
promises of what lies
between the snows and the first
crocus of March.
There is hope.
It waits in the warming earth
and our cooperation
is the only thing required.

After the Election

Let me signal to the crows
that I'm open, safe for
conversation in whatever
language suits a crow or
for that matter
suits the deer
who show up at dusk
knowing it's safe now
to feed.

And open to my neighbor
after the election, after all
the losing and winning.
We just forget
being on different sides,
go back to sharing
gardening tips across the fence,
agree not to worry
about the limelight or
the dim light, about
how to cue attention like a
politician, agree
to live in whatever light
is in the moment,
shining here,
where the trees are finally ready
for a few months' sleep.

A Valentine for Ash Wednesday Falling on February 14, AD 2024

We are stardust.

—JONI MITCHELL

Today we make room
for two occasions joined,
one fixed on calendars,
    in day planners,
        always the same,
            year after year,
one a moving feast,
    shifting
        the way the moon shifts,
and carries its fullness
to a different day each month.

Is it random,
this conjunction of fixed and shifty or
perhaps deliberate,
    from an unseen hand?
To every thing there is a season,
a time for reflection,
    as now,
        this gift,
a day to look more closely
at valentines and ash, how they
    might be connected,
        might be reminders
of what we who celebrate
are made of,
    the dust
        of earth,
the love
    that made the stars.

The Calendar

If, as Scarlett says, tomorrow
is another day, and if time
is an ever-rolling stream
how can I tell one day
from another? Is this,
just another day?
Scarlett returns to Tara,
farms the plantation with
help from Mammy, a slave
no longer on a day that was
yesterday's tomorrow. They
did not put things off 'til
another day, knowing seedtime
won't wait on thoughts of planting.
Or, so it seems, as I try
to catch up on email,
those day markers
that tell me I'm
running out of tomorrows.
I've exhausted myself,
cleaning cupboards that haven't
been disturbed since Vietnam or
was it Watergate?
The family calendar needs updating.
I must see to it now,
before I lose another day.

A Certain Point

He tried to stabilize his core.
"It's what I do," he said,
speaking slowly,
"to avoid a fall."
He was at a certain point,
after talking to the woods,
the mountains. And those clouds
above the sea.
It might have been
the vanishing point,
a point of balance or,
"Is it the edge,"
he said, "here
where I have nothing left
to say, no need
except to listen?"
And to pay attention,
from his stable core,
to what is past memory,
in the silence of the vineyard,
a fleet of invisible spores
floating, the garlic bulb
he kneels now to plant
in the stable earth,
the waiting core,
of his garden.

What Binds Us to History

Like the Rossetta Stone, the Pyramids,
Stonehenge, whatever draws the tourists—
rock binds us to history.
But can we truly know the story
told in stone?

In the great cathedrals, just kids
to Giza and Stonehenge,
the columns of stone talk to the
heavens and would talk to us,
would tell us of more than masons,
their wives and families.
Have we learned to listen?

History is like that, stories held
deep in stone, waiting for us,
who are dulled by what's present,
our vision narrowed to our phones,
our web browsers.
We go to TikTok, thinking
we've got the stories while the stones
do what even trees can't do.
They just sit still.

There is a simple boulder,
a glacier's erratic signature,
young in time as kept by the stars.
It sits on a beach in Maine,
a short beach,
not a half mile long,
but to the sand
no such measurement as miles,
or what we call time,
means anything, and the boulder
is indifferent.

What might it say,
that glacier's memento,
what stories might we hear,
we children of earth,
as we stare at the sea,
while the waves
crash around us.

VI

IV

Unfinished Picture

So here's a question, what
was that old Chevy doing
in the woods and
why had someone shot three holes
in the hood?
Was it frustration,
after a day of hunting,
fully armed, fully camouflaged
with no six-point buck
and bragging rights?
At day's end there was
this unfinished picture
in the woods.
Here was game of a sort,
a rusting car someone had thought
the forest would take care of,
that the trees would hide
better than any junkyard.
And the trees were doing their best,
piling dead leaves on the rotting seats,
sending saplings up
through holes in the floor pans.
But the work wasn't done. The hunter
picked up his Winchester
and finished the picture.

INFLAMED

It could be the crowd
at Caesar's funeral or
any political rally
shouting death to some
presumed traitor, some poor
group huddled in a dark
corner of the nation.
It could be someone
caught in a private passion,
desire that blots
all kindness, or an anger
overwhelming mercy, blind
to the blood and bruising.
It could be no more than
someone's inflamed knees
as she limps into the kitchen
to pour a cup of tea.

The River Is Not Responsible

There are days when anxiety looms,
threatens memory,
    memory of something loved,
        in boyhood or,
            even now,
among the clouds and hills of age.
Memory is the perfect wave,
beautiful as it curls over,
eager for the beach
before it destroys itself on the sand.
And all one wanted was
a faithful replication
of what one had,
before it became memory.
Those loves—the smell of meadow
after mowing, heat of pine forest
in the August afternoon.
Love of the river which, after all,
can't be held responsible—
I let them go.
Become memory they
are fickle, as the river,
    alive to its flowing,
        keeps telling me.

Silent in a Winding

Dorothy was right,
we know.
There is no place
like home,

nothing more
home-like than a
Kansas dirt farm
in tornado season,

with grey-faced Em and Henry.
Home can look different
on different days,
like the day when I

sat with my back
against an ancient
anciently fragrant
white pine or another day

in a canoe, silent
in a winding of
a salt marsh
at high tide.

Dorothy knew home
when her heart
was broken
by absence, by

fear, and the grip
of mortality.
Is there really
a place like home?

I listen to the tree,
the marsh, wait
for my own heart to break,
and for the road home.

Deeply Hidden

The death moth
lives somehow
in the body,
a parasite
eating its slow dinner.

A tiny chrysalis
lying in some safe
warm cavern
of the abdomen,
or in the heart itself.

Some convenient shelter
where the pupa can grow
with no threat
of predator,
sharp beaked and hungry.

Death is like that,
deeply hidden from
the ruddy, the fleet
and sure-footed
who consume life carelessly,

who ignore
whatever might grow,
alert and silent,
safely lodged
somewhere inside them.

Out of Bounds

After the equinox, the bricks
outside the bathroom window cool
and beetles navigate the warmth
that runs from casement cracks
to tempt them from the trees.

Thinking they've found beetle Valhalla
they throw caution to the cold,
fall heedless in the tub
and pay the price of heat:
a Sisyphean bout with sheer

porcelain, bullied by random
bursts of fury from the shower.
I take a seat and watch
an elder of the beetle nation,
tuxed in jet, orange-trimmed,

a blackbird reincarnated
as blackbird prey, now escaped
inside, and staggering against
an enemy without face or wings.
I could play God,

redeem him from pit to floor,
where he could walk for hours, days
before he hit another wall,
one with footholds and ceiling access,
across the Sahara of the living room—

but no, these bugs offend the gods.
Roaches know they belong in cracks,
dash straight to darkness: beetles yaw
through carpet, ignorant of light,
untimely warm. Doomed without leaves.

That Death Is Looking

I know it sounds morbid,
to sit on a quiet
October afternoon and think
that Death is looking
and will,
sooner or later,
find me.
Death neither proud
nor black and sinister,
scythe in hand, no,
nor easeful, in quiet night song.
More the long-lost lover who,
after wandering the alleys,
looking in dumpsters,
peering through grime-coated
back windows, remembers
my favorite haunts,
of shore and meadow,
of forest shadows, or just this
plain room with
a few books, pictures, this
soft furniture, remembers
my habit of sitting still,
and strangely joyful . . .
remembers where to find me,
and at the right time.

Content to Pause

We were in Spokane when
the car overheated
outside the Burger King.
There was nothing to do but wait
while the tired engine slept.
So we waited, backs against
the old Chevy, staring at the parking lot
the Styrofoam and cardboard
piling up around the trash cans.
The baby slept in his car seat
as the afternoon advanced so slowly
we hardly noticed the shadows of the trees
growing longer as the light faded
over the inland plateau.
We knew we'd have to get up,
find someplace for the night,
but not now, not as long as
our journey was content to pause
and catch its breath.

Settled for the Night

On that wide water
between two harbors,
tired and starting to feel
the evening chill,
we saw the porpoises
leap and disappear.
The boat kept steady pace
with whatever swam below
while the sun set,
and the island gulls
settled for the night
on the roofs of our town.

Envoy: Lyric, Sometimes Quiet

A song might be no more
than someone's breath in your ear,
the clinking of a knife
in a jam jar.
The fire in the stove
is said to sing, or even the old clock.
That storm last night ripped
a crazy arm from the big maple.
It lies across the driveway
waiting for the saw, but
it hummed while yielding to the wind.
Listen, we said
as we lay together in the dark,
meaning the wind but
it was really the tree that sang
in the quiet violence of air,
which was itself a kind of song,
along with all singing things—
sunlight, snow melting on a roof,
the plaster of old walls cracking,
the ploughman in the painting,
dividing the earth without a sound.